OPEN EMBRACE

OPEN EMBRACE

A Protestant Couple Rethinks Contraception

BY

Sam & Bethany Torode

WITH A FOREWORD BY

J. Budziszewski

WILLIAM B. EERDMANS PUBLISHING COMPANY

GRAND RAPIDS, MICHIGAN · CAMBRIDGE, U.K.

Published 2002 by Wm. B. Eerdmans Publishing Co.
255 Jefferson Ave. S.E., Grand Rapids, Michigan 49503 /
P.O. Box 163, Cambridge CB3 9PU U.K.

Printed in the United States of America

06 05 04 03 02   5 4 3 2 1

ISBN 0-8028-3973-8

Visit the authors' Web site: www.torodedesign.com

IN GRATITUDE
THIS BOOK IS INSCRIBED
TO OUR PARENTS

The opening in and out,
Body yielding body:
the breaking
through which the new
comes, perching
above its shadow . . .
bud opening to flower
opening to fruit opening
to the sweet marrow
of the seed. . . .

— WENDELL BERRY,
from "The Broken Ground"

CONTENTS

Part Two

Part Three

Foreword

BY J. BUDZISZEWSKI

EVANGELICALS in search of God's teaching turn first to holy Scripture, and that is well and good. But Scripture teaches that God has also built wisdom into the design of his creation, and this is something that evangelicals tend to forget. "By wisdom the LORD laid the earth's foundations," teaches Proverbs, "by understanding he set the heavens in place; by his

J. Budziszewski is an associate professor in the departments of government and philosophy at the University of Texas at Austin.

knowledge the deeps were divided, and the clouds let drop the dew" (3:19–20).[1] We are commanded to pay attention to this wisdom, and in another passage, the command becomes a warning. Wisdom herself is speaking: "Now then, my sons, listen to me; blessed are those who keep my ways. Listen to my instruction and be wise; do not ignore it. . . . For whoever finds me finds life and receives favor from the LORD. But whoever fails to find me harms himself; all who hate me love death" (8:32–33, 35–36).

What could it mean to listen to the wisdom in God's creation? We have examples: "Go to the ant, you sluggard; consider its ways and be wise! It has no commander, no overseer or ruler, yet it stores its provisions in summer and gathers its food at harvest" (6:6–8). How might despising this wisdom lead to death? We have examples of that too, for the previous lesson concludes, "A little sleep, a little slumber, a little folding of the hands to rest — and poverty will come on you like a bandit and scarcity like an armed man" (6:10–11).

I think we get the point about the ant. The question for our time is whether we can get the point about other things in God's creation.

Other things like sex.

Conjugal sex serves not just one great good but three, and they need marriage to come into their own. First among these goods is procreation: God told Adam and Eve to "be fruitful and multiply." This was part of their lordship of the earth. Second is union: When Adam was lonely, God didn't give him a man, an animal, or a crowd of people, but a woman — different from him, yet made with him in God's image. When he saw her he was so astonished that he cried, "This is now bone of my bones and flesh of my flesh" (Genesis 2:23). The third, or sacramental, good of conjugal sex becomes real only when the spouses are united to Christ, for they become a living emblem of his sacrificial love for the Church and the Church's adoring response. Paul is so awed by this that he calls matrimony one of God's secrets. "This mystery is a profound one," he says, "and I am saying that it refers to Christ and the church" (Ephesians 5:32 RSV).

These three goods — procreative, unitive, and sacramental — are a package deal. Our time has made several great errors about them. The first is trying to tear them apart. It doesn't work; they are fused by God's natural and supernatural design, and what God has joined, no man can put asunder. That doesn't stop people from trying.

For example, some wives and husbands try to sever the procreative dimension from the unitive. They imagine that by refusing the "burden" of children, they can achieve a better partnership, a higher intimacy. The problem here is that their partnership was *designed* for raising children, and any so-called intimacy which is deliberately closed to new life is merely a collaboration in selfishness. Children change us in a way we desperately need to be changed. They wake us up, they wet their diapers, they depend on us. Willy-nilly, they knock us out of our selfish habits and force us to live sacrificially for others;

they are the necessary and natural continuation of the shock to our selfishness which is initiated by marriage itself. To be sure, the spouses can live sacrificially for each other, but by itself this love turns too easily inward; married folk who refuse to offer themselves to God for the gift of children are changed only from a pair of selfish Me's to a single selfish Us. By saying "yes" to union but "no" to procreation, we still get a kind of union, but it goes bad; it ferments, turns sour, and begins to stink.

Other wives and husbands try to sever the procreative dimension from the sacramental. They think that by refusing the "distraction" of family, their marriage will become more spiritual, more pure. It would be easier to understand such an attitude in any religion but ours. When Jesus teaches us to call God the Father, do we suppose he is making a joke? What we call distraction, God calls gift — an opportunity to become more like him. We need to take more seriously the teaching that God is *the* Father, the uncreated Father, the model for created fathers. We imagine that he is called Father because he is vaguely like a father;

no, fathers are called fathers because they are vaguely like him. Add to that the fact that he is also the Son and that he chose to have an earthly mother, and family takes on transcendent importance. Some people are called by God to singleness, and for them he has other provisions. But a marriage is the seed of a family; to deny that seed germination is an act of stunning defiance.

Another great error of our age is ignoring the design of the procreative power itself. It's true, of course, that even when spouses welcome children, there may be grave reasons to delay conception. But God has taken care of that already. So deeply has he wrought his purposes into us that a woman's body not only bears fruit, but has seasons — spring, summer, fall, and winter, once every cycle of the moon — providing not only for bringing babies forth, but for spacing them. There is no need to thwart the design, to artificially block fertility during a naturally fertile time. One only has to wait for a few days. If that is too difficult for us, something is wrong.

It might be asked, "Whether we hinder or cooperate with

the times and seasons of our bodies, what difference does it make? The end is the same, whatever the means." But God cares about not only our ends but also our means; he expects us to honor not only his purposes but his arrangements. Doing so brings unexpected graces, some of which are described in this book. Failure to do so brings unexpected harms, and some of these, too, are described.

Speaking of the book. I wish I had read something like it when I was young, and I am glad that it was written by the Torodes. G. K. Chesterton wrote, "It ought to be the oldest things that are taught to the youngest people."[2] Sometimes the oldest things must be taught *by* the youngest people, provided they have learned well from the older ones who taught them. Sam and Bethany have this qualification. They claim no originality, but they have been married long enough to confirm that the oldest things about conjugal love are true, and they are young enough to retain the excitement of the discovery. I cannot imagine better missionaries.

From now on, if anyone supposes that ancient wisdom kills youthful romance, I will simply point to them. My generation pioneered in forgetting the oldest things. Perhaps theirs will pioneer in remembering them.

Preconceived Notions

"DEARLY BELOVED," the minister began, "we are gathered together here in the sight of God, and in the face of this congregation, to join together this man and this woman in holy matrimony."

The congregation was silent in rapt attention, except for the occasional cry of a disgruntled baby with little interest in the sacred occasion at hand.

"Marriage is an honorable estate," the minister continued, "and not to be entered into lightly, but reverently and soberly, duly considering the causes for which matrimony was ordained."

"First, it was ordained for the procreation of children."

At this point, a guest later reported, the calm was interrupted by an involuntary snort of disapproval — "humpf!" — from one of our relatives, who crossed her arms in dismay at such an archaic notion.

That snort summed up a good deal of modern thought on childbearing. In the United States and western Europe, married couples are having fewer and fewer children,[1] thanks in large part to the wide availability of contraceptives, along with the rise of dual careerism in marriages.

Growing up, neither of us was taught to oppose contraception on principle. Sam knew that the Catholic Church officially forbids it, but assumed this was a superstition left over from the Middle Ages. Birth control was never mentioned in his Baptist church. In high school, his friends ridiculed the Catholic position — for them it was enough to quote the lyrics from Monty Python's satirical song, "Every Sperm is Sacred."

One afternoon in college, a friend of Sam's remarked that

she had just read an article explaining why the pope was so opposed to contraception. "I still don't agree with him," she said, "but I was surprised that he actually *had* reasons." Sam's curiosity was piqued, and he decided to research the subject for himself. But, with no prospects for marriage in the near future, he didn't give it too much thought.

As a teenager, Bethany occasionally discussed contraception with her best friend. Though her mom had taught her to be wary of the Pill and other hormonal contraceptives, Bethany still argued in favor of barrier methods such as condoms. At age sixteen, she volunteered at a Crisis Pregnancy Center staffed by women from a variety of church backgrounds. She was surprised to learn that they didn't recommend any form of contraception, not even condoms, for their married clients. Instead, the staff counseled women to become aware of their fertility cycle and to use natural ways of spacing births. After receiving a folder on these natural methods during her training, Bethany promptly slid the information under her bed and thought, "I'll figure out what I believe about all this later."

The time to figure out exactly what we believed about contraception came sooner than either of us expected. We met in January of 2000, became engaged in May, and married in November. During our courtship, the topics of birth control and having children came up early in conversation. We wanted to make wise decisions in these areas and knew that the issue of contraception wouldn't go away by ignoring it.

Unfortunately, we could find little wisdom on the subject from our fellow Protestants. In most of the popular Christian relationship guides, it is simply assumed that couples will be using contraception and that this does not affect their marriage or "sex life." James Dobson, director of Focus on the Family, wrote a book with the promising title *Complete Marriage and Family Home Reference Guide*; but, disappointingly, it does not address the subject of contraception within marriage.

Our experience was not unique. Kevin Offner, a friend of ours who works with InterVarsity Christian Fellowship, was equally frustrated by the lack of critical discernment on this topic. "When I was engaged," he said, "I wanted to think through the whole issue of birth control, so I consulted my married evangelical friends. To a person, they all said, 'Sure, of course we use birth control.' When I asked them why, bringing up the concerns other Christians have, many of them answered, 'You know, I never thought about that!'"

By the time we were engaged, it was clear to us that for love to flourish, we had to grow in knowledge of and respect for each other's bodies — not just our minds and souls. Thanks to a little thing called PMS, Sam quickly realized that understanding the female fertility cycle is not an option — it's a vital part of learning how to love your spouse. You ignore it at your peril. He wondered: Why shouldn't the fertility cycle be respected when it comes to sex? Why shouldn't husbands conform their desires and actions to the natural rhythms of their wives' bodies, rather than ignoring or suppressing them? We decided it was time to look into those natural means of child spacing.

We enrolled in a Natural Family Planning (NFP) home study course offered by the Couple to Couple League. Sorting through all the information was a bit daunting at first, but the more we read, the easier it became to grasp. (In hindsight, we know the best way to learn NFP is from a teacher, not a book. But at the time, we mistakenly thought that a group class would be too embarrassing.) By studying NFP, we learned far more about our bodies' complementary designs than we had ever been taught by doctors or health instructors. More than that, we were prompted to communicate with each other on a deeper level than before and were immersed in what we found to be a profound, biblical perspective on the meaning of sex. Learning NFP is the best way we can imagine to prepare for marriage.

Initially, we were interested in NFP because we hoped to avoid having a baby right away. Though we both love children and want to have a passel of them (whether by birth or by adoption), we figured it would be best to wait until Bethany had finished college. That was the advice we were given.

But as our wedding day approached, we found ourselves more and more looking forward to having a child, and we decided not to put off having a baby for our own convenience or because we were afraid our marriage was not yet ready for such a test. God's timing is different for every couple, and some have legitimate reasons for postponing children immediately after marriage, but we did not. We knew this was a responsibility to be approached with fear and trembling but believed that by inviting new life we would grow closer in ways we had yet to fathom. Love, we discovered, cannot be contained in just two bodies.

In a culture where contraception is so widely accepted, it's easy for Christians like us to grow up and even get married without ever hearing the opposing view. As we researched the existing Christian literature on birth control, we hoped to find a book that we could hand to our friends, one that concisely presented the case against contraception and in favor of Natural Family Planning from a Protestant perspective. Because we couldn't find such a book, we decided to write one.

To avoid certain misunderstandings, we'd like to note a few things at the outset. First, a definition: by "contraception" we mean any process, device, or action whose purpose is to prevent the meeting of sperm and egg when a couple engages in intercourse. This includes things like condoms, diaphragms, and spermicidal jellies, as well as male and female sterilization. Some drugs and devices are commonly referred to as contraceptives but work *after* conception occurs, by preventing a human embryo from implanting in the wall of the uterus. These are properly called abortifacients, since they cause early abortions.

We aren't concerned here with the question of whether contraception, as defined above, is intrinsically evil or sinful. We would say that it's *not ideal*. Rather than pointing fingers, we want to point to a better way.

We also don't make any recommendations about family size.

How many children a particular family can support is a matter between each couple and God. Circumstances vary widely; some couples will be called to larger families, others to smaller. That said, we should try to remain open and generous, careful to discern between God's voice and what our culture tells us about the "ideal" family size.

Though we use our story as a starting point, this book is not about "us" or "our experience." Little of what we have to say is original — most of the ideas in this book were gleaned from wise men and women through the ages. We are not examples to be followed. We are fellow pilgrims, striving to walk the path described in these pages.

We've been questioned as to whether we're too young to write this book. Admittedly, it seems presumptuous for young newlyweds to tackle such a complex issue. But if we're old enough to decide whether or not to use contraception, we can't be too young to share our findings and conclusions with others. We wish that the arguments against contraception were widely known. We wish that a significant number of more experienced Protestants were providing young Christians with sound guidance and information on birth control. If that were the case, we would gladly step aside and let others speak.

Though we don't have years of experience to back up the conclusions presented here, experience is not an inherently good thing. Old age can bring wisdom and discernment; it can also bring hardness and an unwillingness to change. Youth can bring ignorance and blind idealism; it can also bring freshness and innocence.

Before we were married, we researched and weighed the arguments for and against contraception solely on their merits. Being Protestants, we had no need to make our decisions conform to any one church's teaching, though we have learned to respect deeply the historic position of the Catholic Church.

Every couple should reach a mutual decision on contraception based on prayer, Scripture reading, and solid reasoning. If you disagree with the arguments presented in this book, you should be able to articulate and defend your reasons for doing so. We're open to hearing such disagreements. Whatever your conclusions, we hope our efforts will prove helpful to your own moral discernment.

Finally, a note on style. From time to time, we use the word *man* to refer to all human beings. For example, when we write "man is a unity of soul and body" or (quoting Scripture) "God created man in his image," this includes both men and women. No reader belonging to the human race should feel left out.

PART ONE

God created man in His own image, in the image of God He created him; male and female He created them. God blessed them; and God said to them, "Be fruitful and multiply, and fill the earth, and subdue it. . . ."

— GENESIS 1:27–28

When husband and wife are united in marriage they no longer seem like something earthly, but rather like the image of God himself.

— ST. JOHN CHRYSOSTOM

Imago Dei

WHAT DOES IT MEAN to be a human being? For Christians, it means to be created in the image of God. But what exactly is *that* supposed to mean?

This may seem an odd question with which to begin a discussion of contraception, but it's really the most important question of all. Our answer to this question determines how we view ourselves, how we relate to each other, and even how we approach the subject of birth control.

Another word for *image* is *icon*. In the age of computers, we're very familiar with the concept of icons. Click on an icon for a program, and the program boots up; click on an icon for a file, and the file opens. Because we each bear the image of God, we are all icons of God. Whatever you do to another person, you ultimately do to God himself. Jesus said, "Truly I say to you, to the extent that you did it to one of these brothers of Mine, even the least of them, you did it to Me" (Matthew 25:40).

All of creation is suffused with the glory of God, but God bestowed his image on man alone. Only man possesses reason, free will, and an immortal soul. Our bodies, too, carry the divine image. "The word Man," says St. Gregory Palamas, "is not applied to either soul or body separately, but to both together, since together they have been created in the image of God."[1] Since it's inseparable from our bodies, even our sexuality reflects God's likeness; from the very beginning, man was a sexual being, created male and female, and blessed with fertility.

How can our sexuality bear witness to the image of God in man? For starters, God himself is a "family" — a Trinity of three Persons. Human sexuality allows us to participate in families and communities of our own. As God declared when he brought Eve out of Adam, differentiating man into male and female, "It is not good for the man to be alone" (Genesis 2:18).

The Trinity is the perfect example of selfless, life-creating love. Married persons are called to participate in this love in a special way: through the marital embrace. Through sex, the love of husband and wife can become incarnate in the co-creation with God of a new human person — a child never before seen on this earth. Our money bears the image of Caesar. How much more valuable are our children, who bear the image of God? Every one is unique, invaluable, and irreplaceable: "For you formed my inward parts; You wove me in my mother's womb. I will give thanks to you, for I am fearfully and wonderfully made" (Psalm 139:13–14).

Each of us is a priceless original, hand-fashioned by the Creator. Our countenance, our body shape, our unique combination of hair, eye, and skin colors — they are exclusive to us. These little facets reflect the beauty of the Creator as a prism reflects light. "Faced with the sacredness of life and of the human person," Pope John Paul II asserts, ". . . wonder is the only appropriate attitude."[2]

Can any of us fully grasp this truth? Each person we encounter is created in the image of God. Each is of infinite value. None deserves to be exploited — used as a means to an end. The only response appropriate to a fellow person is love.

"In order to find God," writes the Greek Orthodox bishop Kallistos Ware, "we do not have to leave the world, to isolate ourselves from our fellow human beings, and to plunge into some kind of mystical void. On the contrary, Christ is looking at us through the eyes of all those whom we meet. Once we recognize his universal presence, all our acts of practical service to others become acts of prayer."[3]

Sex, too, ought to be an act of prayer, a joyous song of praise to the Creator. Because sexual love can express what is best in us, it is also vulnerable to the worst corruption. As sinful human beings, husbands and wives must always be on guard against using each other. We are constantly faced with the choice between treating each other as mere bodies for our own gratification, or reverencing each other as icons of God, windows to heaven. It is a choice between selfishness and selflessness.

This is where we begin our discussion of contraception: in awe of the sacredness of the human person, made in the image of God, worthy of selfless love. In the words of a favorite prayer, "Grant, O Lord, that in loving each other, we may love you yourself."

And He answered and said, "Have you not read that He who created them from the beginning made them male and female, and said, 'For this reason a man shall leave his father and mother and be joined to his wife, and the two shall become one flesh'? So they are no longer two, but one flesh. What therefore God has joined together, let no man separate."

—— MATTHEW 19:4–6

God created Adam and Eve that there may be great love between them, reflecting the mystery of Divine unity.

—— ST. THEOPHILUS OF ANTIOCH

One Flesh

T HE PASTOR who presided at our wedding used the eloquent ceremony from the seventeenth-century Book of Common Prayer. This service gives three purposes of marriage: first, it was instituted for the procreation of children; second, it is a remedy against sin; and third, it provides for the mutual society, help, and comfort of the spouses.

Though all three of these purposes are drawn straight from Scripture, a few of our Christian friends objected to the order in which they were given. They felt that companionship (mutual society) was the most important reason for marriage, and that procreation was a distant second. The point, we replied, is not that one aspect of marriage is more important than another; each is important and none should dominate at the expense of the others.

Procreation, for example, should exist only within the context of self-giving love and companionship. It's wrong to use your spouse for any reason, even for the noble cause of having children. "One does not love in order to have children," explains Russian Orthodox theologian Alexander Schmemann. "Love needs no justification; it is not because it gives life that it is good; it is because it is good that it gives life."[1]

Even so, there is good sense in listing procreation first among the purposes of marriage. It's the umbrella under which the other aspects of marriage are nurtured. Having children (or adopting them) brings husbands and wives closer together and expands the community of love. Sociologists tell us that with each child a couple has, their chances of divorce are significantly reduced, and the strongest predictor of marital stability is the presence of small children in the home.[2] Moreover, the responsibilities, trials, and joys of parenthood are opportunities to cultivate holiness.

God created marriage such that husband and wife become *one flesh*. Jesus expounds upon this teaching when he condemns divorce: "So they are no longer two, but one flesh. What therefore God has joined together, let no man separate" (Matthew 19:6). Sex is the *consummation* of marriage. Because it represents the complete union of husband and wife, it is the physical embodiment of the vows exchanged by a husband and wife on their wedding day. Ecstatic love is transcendent — it leads us out of our selves (the Greek *ekstasis* means "to stand beside one's self"). St. Paul writes that this one-flesh union is of mystical significance — it is a great mystery, a sign of the union of Christ and his Church.

In her novel *Souls Raised from the Dead*, Doris Betts provides a beautiful picture of a one-flesh union. Describing two grandparents, she writes, "A plain and stocky couple, once blond and ruddy, now bleached by the same work and weather and habits, they might have been siblings . . . or resemblance might deepen over the years from steady absorption of each other's bodily fluids. . . . *Ye shall be one flesh.*"[3]

It may seem strange to say that, within marriage, the free exchange of bodily fluids is a means of experiencing the grace of God, but we believe this to be true. As the Bible makes clear, the mystery of marriage is not about becoming one mind or one soul, but one *flesh*, encompassing the totality of man.

From this bodily union, procreation and the greater union of the spouses can result. It's important to remember, however, that *we* don't create children — God does, and they are a gift only he can bestow. As married persons, our part is to remain open to children, by becoming one flesh and refusing to compromise that union. This is not to say that every time a couple makes love, they should be trying to conceive — after all, conception is possible for only a few days of a woman's cycle and impossible during times such as pregnancy and after menopause. But every time husband and wife come together, they ought to do so in earnest, in an open embrace, withholding nothing from each other — including their fertility. By participating in marital relations, they should be indicating their willingness to accept whatever naturally follows; during the fertile times of a woman's cycle, this may include children.

Respect for the one-flesh mystery of marriage gives us serious qualms about the use of contraception. To invoke St. Paul's analogy, would Christ ever withhold any part of himself from the Church, or sterilize his love? To our minds, anything less than a true one-flesh union fails to represent the completely self-giving love of Christ for the Church. This is why we believe that when a husband and wife have serious reasons to avoid pregnancy, it's better to abstain for a time than to diminish the meaning and mystery of sex.

At some point we began assuming that the life of the body would be the business of grocers and medical doctors, who need take no interest in the spirit, whereas the life of the spirit would be the business of churches, which would have at best only a negative interest in the body.

—— WENDELL BERRY

All loves are bodily, require
that the lips part, and press their trace
of secrecy upon the one
beloved. . . .

—— SCOTT CAIRNS

Body Language

W E'VE READ DEFENSES of contraception from several Christian authors. All agree that when it comes to birth control, it's our *intentions* that matter, not necessarily our actions. Contraceptives, they say, are tools that can be used for good or ill. For example, one such author condemns the abuse of contraception to "facilitate promiscuity" but says that the use of contraception by married Christians "can be a great blessing" because "it permits them time to grow in greater love and commitment at the beginning of marriage."[1] By severing the biological link between sex and procreation, these authors assert, contraception can nurture the spiritual companionship of the spouses.

Underlying these arguments is the assumption that the "spiritual" aspects of sex are more important than, and can be enjoyed apart from, the "merely physical," biological aspect of fertility. The Bible, however, speaks of man as a unity of matter and spirit, a "living soul" — not a holy soul trapped in an evil body, as the ancient heresy of Gnosticism taught. Because man is a unity of soul and body, one can't elevate the soul by subverting the body. Any attempt to do so sets the body against the soul; as a result, the body is reduced to an object. By pitting spirit against matter, and companionship against procreation, contraception can become a means of exploiting the body and using one's spouse — in spite of our good intentions.

With contraception, as with all of life, actions and intentions can't easily be separated. What we do with our bodies, we also do with our souls. The apostle Paul writes of this astonishing truth in 1 Corinthians:

> Do you not know that your bodies are members of Christ? Shall I then take away the members of Christ and make them members of a prostitute? May it never be! . . . Do you not know that your body is a temple of the Holy Spirit who is in you, whom you have from God, and that you are not your own? For you have been bought with a price: therefore glorify God in your body. (1 Corinthians 6:15–20)

Even when our mouths are silent, our bodies are talking; and actions speak louder than words. Our complementary bodies, male and female, were designed so that husbands and wives can give themselves completely to each other. In the language of the body, giving yourself to your spouse in the marital embrace says "I do." Each sex act should be a renewal of the vows we made on our wedding day.

Uniting the male and female bodies in love says something beautiful; it speaks of the union of Christ and the Church. Lovemaking should always be life-giving, even when it does not generate new life in the form of a child. The procreative partnership of a husband and wife goes far beyond the conception of children. Human sexual desire is not limited to the times we are fertile — we were designed to express our love sexually even when conception is impossible. But while sex is not solely for conception, it is not our place to deliberately separate sex from its procreative aspect.

How does contraception alter the language of our bodies? Regardless of our intent, deliberately withholding or subverting our fertility during sex sends a message: "I am not giving myself completely to my spouse," or, "I will not accept my spouse in his entirety." When we should be saying "I do," contraception says "I do not."

Christian proponents of contraception often assert that

while a marriage on the whole should be open to children, each intimate act need not be.[2] What if it was suggested that while a marriage on the whole should be monogamous, each intimate act need not reflect that? Because sex is the consummation, the summing up, of marriage, each intimate act is a picture of the marriage as a whole. If marriage is about completely giving yourself to your spouse, then sex should embody that truth. The issue is not whether each intimate act is able to result in conception. As we noted earlier, a woman is infertile for most of her cycle, and a couple may be infertile for extended periods of time or even indefinitely. This does not mean that intercourse during these times is closed to children in the way that contraception, by placing a barrier between sex and procreation, is closed to children.

Contraception is not explicitly condemned in the Bible, and many Christians equate that silence with approval. But abortion isn't mentioned by name in the Bible, either. In cases like these, we need to think biblically. The contraceptive mentality treats fertility as a sickness and children as inconveniences. Scripture, however, tells us that our bodies, with their fertility, were created good. The Bible teaches us to approach sexual intimacy and the possibility of conception with awe and reverence. The womb is the place where God forms new life in his image, not a frontier to be arrogantly invaded and conquered.

What we do with our bodies tells God what we think of his handiwork. He thought it "very good" — do we? We ought to respect the integrity of our bodies and alter the way they're intended to function as little as possible. This does not mean that all medical technology is bad, only that it should be used in accordance with our nature and dignity as human beings. Because we live in a fallen world, there are occasions when the body is not working right, and medical intervention is necessary to restore it to rightful order. For example, while we were writing this book, Bethany came down with appendicitis. Her appendix was infected and had to be removed in order for her body to function properly. But fertility, unlike appendicitis, is the norm of a healthy body. Pregnancy is not a disease — why vaccinate against it?

You cannot examine the coal away from the fire. You can't learn the meaning of a rose by pulling it to pieces. — ELISABETH ELLIOT

Pleasure is nature's way of encouraging us to do necessary things in themselves not always pleasant. Those who live for pleasure, delighted by the attractive package, throw the gift away — *in this instance of sex, the great gift of life itself.* — JOHN SENIOR

Intended for Pleasure?

ONE MORNING, while on our honeymoon, we dropped into a corner convenience store to buy some snacks. Behind the cashier's counter was an array of condoms. The little boxes had names like Erotica and Bareback and showed air-brushed photos of women in various stages of undress. We tried to imagine a bride's reaction if her husband pulled out a pack of Night Riders. *What a turn on.*

At least, we reflected, the sleazy condom manufacturers are honest. The "classier" brands may have subtler packaging, but the product being sold is the same: the pleasure of sex without the "consequences."

Giving up contraception goes against everything our culture tells us about sex and marriage, and sometimes Christians have a hard time thinking outside of the surrounding culture's assumptions. As G. K. Chesterton once quipped, "I suppose that even Jonah, once he was swallowed, could not see the whale."

Evangelicals are known for "engaging the culture." Contemporary Christian music, for example, often mimics the sound of "secular" music while adding Christian lyrics, as though the music conveys no message of its own. Problems arise when we begin engaging the culture and end up marrying it.

Our culture tells us that sex is really about pleasure, not spousal unity and procreation. Thus, in order to stay culturally relevant, many Christians stress that it was God who designed sex to yield pleasure. From this legitimate starting point, however, some Christians end up elevating pleasure above the procreative and unitive aspects of sex. In so doing, they unconsciously buy into our culture's hedonistic pursuit of pleasure as an end in itself. That sounds strong, but check out the shelves of most Protestant bookstores — you'll find books on sexual technique that rival the pages of *Cosmopolitan.*

Before we began researching birth control, we had no idea that such a genre as the "evangelical sex guide" existed. We made it through the wonderfully awkward first weeks of marriage without heading to the bookstore for expert guidance. Judging by the number of copies sold, however, it appears that a large market for such books exists. *Intended for Pleasure*; *The Gift of Sex*; *The Act of Marriage*; *52 Ways to Have Fun, Fantastic Sex* — the list of best-selling titles goes on. Looking them over, you would think that bedroom virtuosity is the key to experiencing marriage "as God intended."

Since contraception has enabled our culture's pursuit of unfettered sex, it's no surprise that many of the Christian sex guides, like their secular counterparts, sing praises to the Pill. In *The Act of Marriage*, authors Tim and Beverly LaHaye give virtually the same advice on birth control (and much else) found in Dr. Ruth's books. "Because of its safety and simplicity," the LaHayes write, "we consider the pill the preferred method for a new bride in the early stages of marriage. Then, after she and her husband have learned the art of married love, she may decide on some other method."[1]

According to popular evangelical author Tony Campolo, using contraception is one way of "following Jesus without embarrassing God." In his book by that title, Campolo writes,

> God is not against the joy of sex. . . . Just remember that God enjoys having a good time, and God is into sensate pleasures. That's why God created the world and everything in it. It gave God pleasure. It turned God on. . . . I believe that God enjoys having people share all the pleasures of life that God means for them to enjoy within marriage, as long as they enjoy them in the ways in which God intends for them to be enjoyed. . . . That is why I believe that birth control is a good thing. It delivers sex from simply being a

means for creating babies. It frees us up to use sex in this bonding manner. Many opponents of birth control miss the point completely. Once we understand that sex was meant for pleasurable bonding, we are likely to give more attention to how to make sex work for us.[2]

Yes, sex is joyful. Yes, it is pleasurable bonding. But, ironically, if pleasure becomes the focus of our lovemaking, true and lasting pleasure will elude us. What exactly is "pleasure," anyway? Just an intense stimulation of nerve endings? Or that and much more — the knowledge that you are giving yourselves completely, fertility and all, to each other?

In marriage, lovemaking is not about "getting some"; it allows us to be as close as possible to each other — it renews our union. Spousal love is intended to be absolutely self-giving. "Husbands, love your wives, just as Christ also loved the church and gave Himself up for her" (Ephesians 5:25).

All married couples will fall short of Christ's example, whether we use contraception or not. But the pursuit of sexual pleasure apart from the inbuilt procreative aspect of sex can be a major obstacle to a healthy marriage characterized by self-giving love. Bringing drugs and devices into the middle of the marital embrace will not increase our pleasure, rightly understood. Consider this testimony from a Christian couple who, after five years of marriage, gave up contraception:

> During our contraceptive years we worried about "performance" when we engaged in intimacy. We lost sight of what true love really means — giving for the good of the other. Without even realizing it, we were destroying the love/life bond which is so crucial to marriage. We were celebrating the unitive aspect of our relationship, but not the procreative.[3]

In the traditional Christian wedding service, there is no mention of pleasure or feelings. When we exchanged vows, we did not promise, at the deepest level, to give each other goose bumps. Instead, we vowed to remain faithful always, even through hard times, poverty, and sickness. The lasting pleasure to be found in marriage is the fruit of selfless love. Bearing and raising children brings pleasure; establishing a household together brings pleasure; serving each other brings pleasure. All of these things bring sorrow, too. It's hard work, but, in the words of poet and farmer Wendell Berry, "work is the health of love."[4]

To experience the gift of married love while respecting the laws of conception is to acknowledge that one is not master of the sources of life, but rather the minister of the design established by the Creator. —— POPE PAUL VI

In the Family Way

UNDERSTANDABLY, many people fear that by giving up contraception, they'll lose control of their lives and bodies. While Christians believe that our bodies are not our own — they belong to God — we're also called to be good stewards and responsible parents.

It's a common assumption that if couples forego technology and follow the ways of nature, they will end up with fifteen to twenty kids, running down the wife's body in the process. But is that really how God designed our fertility to work?

At least one inbuilt means of child spacing suggests otherwise: breastfeeding. In industrialized nations, where bottles and formula are readily available, most mothers nurse their babies only for a few months, if at all. This is unfortunate because fresh breast milk is the ideal food for at least the first year of a child's life. Moreover, women who breastfeed exclusively (with no use of bottles), frequently, and on demand usually experience an extended period of infertility after childbirth, naturally spacing children about two years apart.[1] Though out of fashion in America, this is the norm in many "undeveloped" parts of the world.

But what about those women who can't breastfeed, or who experience a quicker return of fertility? What if there is a need to space children further apart, or a couple has serious reasons to avoid pregnancy? Other natural ways of child spacing are based on the same principle: respecting God's design for the body by following a woman's natural phases of infertility and abstaining during fertile times.

To most Protestants, the phrase "natural child spacing" means the notoriously unreliable rhythm method. *The Act of Marriage*, for example, discounts the rhythm method as the "least effective" form of birth control and mentions no other natural option.[2] But the rhythm method was superceded decades ago by a scientific, reliable, natural form of child spacing known as Natural Family Planning (NFP). With NFP, couples can identify the days per cycle (generally three to seven) that a wife might become pregnant by monitoring up to three different fertility signs: her body's production of cervical fluid, her oral temperature upon waking, and the position of her cervix. These signs are recorded daily and tracked on a chart. The couple then decides whether to make love during the fertile days or to abstain until they have passed.

In our experience, most Christian doctors and pastors will tell couples that all natural forms of fertility regulation are unreliable for spacing children. A shopworn joke goes, "What do you call people who use natural birth control? Parents." The joke is

not only demeaning of parents and their children, it's also based
on outdated information. Elisabeth Elliot, one of the few well-
known Protestants to promote NFP, has this to say:

> On my radio program I talked about Natural Family
> Planning, and I had several letters from people who told me
> that I made it sound too complicated. One of them told
> how effective natural family planning had been in India.
> Over a 24-month study, less than 1% of all the couples who
> were tested — and there were 96,641 uses of marriage —
> had an unplanned pregnancy over the two years of the
> study. According to standard statistical measures used in
> pregnancy calculations, this translates to an effectiveness
> rate of 99.2% — for a natural, not artificial, method of
> family planning.[3]

Many Protestants have never heard of NFP, or dismiss it
out-of-hand because of its Catholic connotations. But even
non-Christians are beginning to discover its benefits for both
avoiding and achieving pregnancy. While some Christian

guides, such as *The Act of Marriage*, offer misleading advice on fertility regulation, Planned Parenthood's Web site includes a fairly accurate and positive overview of NFP. In fact, one of the only reasons why NFP isn't appropriate for everyone, according to Planned Parenthood, is that it cannot be practiced outside of a loving, committed relationship.

> Charting fertility patterns requires dedication, education, and practice. It is most effective when both partners are mature, responsible, and committed to making them work. That's why it is very important for both partners to learn the fundamentals and support each other in observing the abstinence.[4]

Dedicated, mature, responsible, committed, and supportive of each other. Isn't that an apt description of what Christian spouses should be?

One secular author, Toni Weschler, has been speaking for over twenty years on what she calls the "Fertility Awareness Method"

(FAM). While Weschler does not discourage couples from using condoms during the fertile time, most of what she writes about FAM also applies to NFP.

Weschler's book, *Taking Charge of Your Fertility*, demonstrates that from the perspective of good health alone, NFP makes perfect sense. Becoming aware of the female fertility cycle, she writes,

> is about so much more than merely understanding female hygiene and menstruation. At its core is a philosophy of taking control of, understanding, and demystifying the menstrual cycle and its effects on you.... The self-knowledge available from Fertility Awareness is a valuable resource for all kinds of personal decision making. Perhaps more important, it encourages women to value and trust knowledge provided by their own bodies.
>
> Gynecologists are experts in women's physiology, so it should come as no surprise that most women turn to doctors rather than themselves to interpret their bodies. Reliance on physicians would be understandable if the

knowledge doctors possessed about women's cycles was incomprehensible to the general public. But this is basic fertility, not brain surgery. In reality, this information is quite simple, and not the mystery so many people believe it is.[5]

Perhaps the greatest reward of NFP is the fostering of communication between spouses. The husband is encouraged to learn to follow his wife's cycle, ask questions about her fertility signs, help to chart them, and talk about whether or not to abstain. Weschler elaborates:

> Men are often criticized for not taking a bigger role in birth control or even pregnancy achievement. But the truth is that many men are very caring and loving and would be happy to be more actively involved if only there were a way they could. . . . The beauty of charting is that a man can be as involved as his partner — taking her temps, jotting down her fertility signs, determining when her fertile phase has begun and ended. And rather than perceiving it as work,

most people agree that the minute or two a day is so en-
lightening that it can be fun rather than a chore. Men who
help their partners chart find that they discover a lot about
them in the process. The potential for furthering intimacy
is obvious. As one of my male clients said, "If you can talk
about cervical fluid, you can talk about anything!"[6]

Does NFP strengthen marriages? Marriage counselor Gregory
Popcak believes that it can.

It has been my experience that couples who use NFP are
actually challenged to work harder on having good marriages.
They are challenged to communicate better, to overcome
their personal weaknesses more willingly and generously, and
they are forced to nurture their friendship more because they
can't just "throw sex" at their problems. By way of example, I
have witnessed hundreds of non-NFP couples who couldn't
communicate their way out of a paper bag, who had lost
common interests over the years, who did not really like each
other and were often outright abusive in their treatment of

one another, but then were completely surprised when their partner wanted a divorce. "I thought everything was great! After all, we had sex almost every day!"[7]

Unlike contraception, which can have many harmful side effects, NFP actually has a number of unexpected side benefits. By taking your temperature and tracking your mucus, you may be able to identify irregularities and sicknesses of which you would otherwise be unaware. It helps mitigate PMS by letting you anticipate and alleviate its symptoms (through natural means of adjusting estrogen and progesterone levels such as exercise, changes in diet, vitamins, more sleep, less stress, etc.). It aids in regulating your cycle and enhancing your health and fertility by teaching you how to improve daily habits. Charting your temperature even gives you a reliable way of determining both if you are pregnant and when your baby is due. No hassle with pregnancy tests is required.

Many will object, "But I haven't experienced any side effects from contraception." While you are still using contraception, it isn't always possible to notice its effects. One Protestant woman says this about her own experience of going off the Pill:

> I never *felt* irritable when I was using the Pill. In fact, I had been pleased that I experienced "no" side effects. But in reality, I did; the Pill had produced subtle but serious changes in my body's chemistry and my emotions. We wondered if we had left our friendship at the altar. We had never dreamed that we would fight and argue like we did! We can't bring children into a home like this, we thought. Physical intimacy was no picnic, either, and I felt like a failure. I simply wasn't interested. Ever. Where had all that passion gone that I had struggled to keep in check before we were married? We wondered if we had failed, or if we had simply been cheated. . . .
>
> I quit the Pill, and before we knew it, we were pregnant! But there were other big — and unexpected — changes. We didn't fight anymore. Our relationship blossomed once again. And lovemaking became the delight God meant it to be. I was apprehensive at first; was this just an emotional high in

anticipation of our baby's arrival? But as the months went by, we both knew that a dark cloud had lifted from over our marriage when we threw away the Pill. I told my husband, "*This* is what I always dreamed marriage would be like."[8]

Some may assume that charting fertility signs "takes all the spontaneity out of love," or is "too hard." On the contrary, we can personally attest that charting is not that complicated, and it encourages a deeper understanding of intimacy. This greater comprehension of the wondrous ways our bodies are created actually enhances desire, and learning how truly amazing our reproductive systems are increases one's awe of life.

It is often asked, "What's the difference between NFP and contraception? Don't couples who use either means have the same goal in mind?" The fundamental difference is that NFP, which is simply informed abstinence, respects the female fertility cycle and preserves the integrity and wholeness of each sex act. The one-flesh union is neither diminished nor compromised. Elisabeth Elliot explains:

The distinction that became so clear to me is the difference between the deliberate interruption of the transmis-
sion of life during the fertile period, and the responsible
use of the natural rhythms which are imminent in the
reproductive system. In other words, the difference between
impeding a natural process, or making legitimate use of
the natural disposition which God the Creator has built
into the reproductive system.[9]

Because it requires that couples give up sex during the fertile
time to avoid conception, NFP is based on self-sacrifice. When
couples fast from sex in order to space their children, they are
reminded both of the goodness of lovemaking and of God's
purposes in creating it. It's like fasting from food, which is both
a spiritual discipline and a way of maintaining good health.
Contraception, on the other hand, could be compared to binging
and purging. It promises to satisfy our appetite for sex while
ignoring its created purpose. The promise is an empty one.

As the Book of Ecclesiastes says, there is "a time to embrace, and a time to refrain from embracing" (3:5 KJV). It's up to each couple, in prayerful cooperation with God, to determine the proper times. Following the fertility cycle with NFP is very helpful for our discernment. But however good, NFP can be misued by always abstaining during the fertile times and avoiding children for selfish reasons. It's also important to remember the apostle Paul's admonition to those who take abstinence within marriage to an extreme. A wife has authority over her huband's body, and a husband has authority over his wife's; therefore, only abstain "by mutual consent and for a time, so that you may devote yourselves to prayer. Then come together again so that Satan will not tempt you . . ." (1 Corinthians 7:5 NIV).

We don't like to call NFP a "method of birth control." That might give the false impression that NFP is just another tool for couples to use in spacing children, but it is both more challenging and more rewarding than that. It is better described as a way of life, one that must be embarked upon in order to be fully understood and appreciated.

PART TWO

Sam

So then, brethren, stand firm and hold to the traditions which you were taught, whether by word of mouth or by letter from us.

— 2 THESSALONIANS 2:15

Tradition may be defined as an extension of the franchise. Tradition means giving votes to the most obscure of all classes, our ancestors. It is the democracy of the dead. Tradition refuses to submit to the small and arrogant oligarchy of those who happen to be walking about.

— G. K. CHESTERTON

Of Trains & Tradition

O N H I S R A D I O P R O G R A M, Garrison Keillor likes to tell the story of an old Catholic priest in Lake Wobegon, Minnesota: "His philosophy on birth control and abortion was, 'If you didn't want to go to Minneapolis, why did you get on the train?'"

In an age bent on separating sex and procreation, there's a lot of wisdom in that simple statement. Janet Smith, one of the foremost advocates of NFP, remarks that, when faced with an unplanned pregnancy, couples will often ask, *What went wrong?*

How did this happen? What has happened, of course, is that something has gone *right*. Making love has resulted in making a baby — that's how it was designed to work.

The evangelists of birth control would like us to believe that we've finally separated the "pleasure" of sex from the "danger" of procreation. The prophets of reproductive technology, meanwhile, preach that human life can be generated just as well in a petri dish as in the womb, or better. As one doctor proclaims, "I think we're going to begin to view our children as just too damn important to leave to just some random meeting of sperm and egg."[1] But the connection between sex and procreation can never truly be broken. It is written into the structure of reality, and our attempts to act otherwise will only end in misery.

Nevertheless, the quest to separate sex from fertility is centuries old. Historian Andrea Tone writes:

The oldest guide to contraception, the *Petrie Papyrus*, an Egyptian medical papyrus dating to 1850 B.C., recommended vaginal suppositories made of crocodile dung, gum, or a mixture of honey and sodium carbonate. Aristotle, writing in the fourth century B.C., noted the tendency of women of his day to coat their cervixes with olive oil before intercourse. Women in preindustrial West Africa made intravaginal plugs of crushed root, Japanese women made tampons of bamboo tissue, and women of Easter Island made algae and seaweed pessaries. (A pessary is a substance or device inserted into the vagina that blocks, repels, or otherwise neutralizes sperm.) [2]

The early Christians faced a contraceptive culture not unlike ours today. Around A.D. 100, just a few decades after St. Paul wrote his letter to the Ephesians, an Ephesian doctor named Soranos authored a gynecological textbook describing seventeen methods of contraception, which he recommended as a safer option than abortion.[3] From the start, however, the Church insisted that sexuality and fertility were part of a continuous harmony, and that "what God has joined together, let no man separate." For that reason, not only abortion but also contraception was universally condemned.

St. Hippolytus (c. 225) strongly rebuked Christian women who "use drugs of sterility or bind themselves tightly in order to expel a fetus which has already been engendered."[4] Epiphanius of Salamis (c. 375) wrote against certain Egyptian heretics who "prevent the conceiving of children."[5] St. John Chrysostom (c. 391) preached, "that which is sweet, and universally desirable, the having of children, they esteem grievous and unwelcome. Many with this view have even paid money to be childless, and have mutilated nature, not only killing the newborn, but even acting to prevent their beginning to live."[6] Chrysostom asked, "Why do you sow where the field is eager to destroy the fruit, where there are medicines of sterility, where there is murder before birth?"[7]

It was not until the twentieth century that birth control became a "Catholic issue"; before then, it was a concern of all Christians. The father of the Reformation, Martin Luther, lamented, "How great, therefore, the wickedness of human nature is! How many girls there are who prevent conception and kill and expel tender fetuses, although procreation is the work of God!"[8] John Calvin and John Wesley were unwavering in their opposition to both abortion and contraception.

In 1930, the Anglican Church became the first Christian body to approve the "cautious" use of contraceptives. Not long after, nearly all the Protestant denominations abandoned the ancient Christian teaching on contraception.

If we believe that the Church is guided by the Holy Spirit and yet we approve of the use of contraception, this should give us pause. How could the universal Church have been so mistaken about this issue for so many years? Was it the leading of the Holy Spirit, or the spirit of the age, that caused Christians to change?

There is a way which seems right to a man, but its end is the way of death.

— PROVERBS 16:25

In loving the husband and wife must turn the attention to each other, as happens in Natural Family Planning, and not to self, as happens in contraception. Once that living love is destroyed by contraception abortion follows very easily.

— MOTHER TERESA

From Contraception to Abortion

A STORY in the January 2001 issue of *National Geographic* reports on the excavation of the ancient city Ashkelon, the great metropolis of the biblical Philistines. One photo shows an oil-burning lamp embellished with an image of two bodies united in intercourse. Not far from where the lamp and many other erotic artifacts were discovered, the article explains, archaeologists found a sewer filled with the skeletons of discarded infants, likely the progeny of temple prostitutes. Then, as now, a culture that worships sex without procreation will sacrifice its children.

In America's history, there has been a clear progression from endorsing contraception to accepting abortion. Legally, "reproductive rights" were first established by the Supreme Court in *Griswold v. Connecticut* (1965), which guaranteed the right to contraception for married persons. In *Eisenstadt v. Baird* (1972), the Court extended contraceptive rights to the unmarried. Both decisions overturned state laws, passed by largely Protestant legislatures in the nineteenth century, banning or restricting the sale of contraceptives. In so doing, they set the precedent for the right to abortion created by *Roe v. Wade* (1973).

On the surface, it seems ridiculous: How could the right to prevent pregnancy be construed as a right to terminate a pregnancy? Writing for the majority in *Roe*, Justice Harry Blackmun stated that the realm of "sexual privacy" established by *Griswold* and *Eisenstadt* "is broad enough to encompass a woman's decision whether or not to terminate her pregnancy."[1]

Perhaps the greatest reason that the widespread acceptance of contraception led to the legalization of abortion is that abortion is often used as a backup for contraceptive failure. If a woman didn't *intend* to get pregnant, the argument goes, why should she be forced to continue with the pregnancy? This is wrong; we must be responsible for our actions regardless of our intentions. But this mentality is so entrenched in our society that it is unlikely abortion will be outlawed as long as most couples rely on contraception. Too many people have built their lives around the availability of contraception and, if that fails, abortion. This is exactly what the Supreme Court argued when upholding *Roe v. Wade* in *Planned Parenthood v. Casey* (1992):

> [The *Roe v. Wade* decision] could not be repudiated without serious inequity to people who, for two decades of economic and social developments, have organized intimate relationships and made choices that define their views of themselves and their places in society, in reliance on the availability of abortion in the event that contraception should fail. . . .
>
> It should be recognized, moreover, that in some critical respects, the abortion decision is of the same character as the decision to use contraception, to which *Griswold v. Connecticut, Eisenstadt v. Baird,* and *Carey v. Population Services*

International afford constitutional protection. We have no doubt as to the correctness of those decisions. They support the reasoning in *Roe* relating to the woman's liberty, because they involve personal decisions concerning not only the meaning of procreation but also human responsibility and respect for it.[2]

I doubt that very many Christians would seek an abortion if their contraception failed. But because the Protestant churches, beginning in the 1930s, endorsed contraception and encouraged its acceptance in our culture, they helped prepare the way for *Roe v. Wade*. In fact, the *Roe* Court specifically cited the beliefs of Protestant Christians to support its decision:

It should be sufficient to note briefly the wide divergence of thinking on this most sensitive and difficult question. There has always been strong support for the view that life does not begin until live birth. It appears to be the predominant, though not the unanimous, attitude of the Jewish faith. It may be taken to represent also the position of a large segment of the

Protestant community, insofar as that can be ascertained; organized groups that have taken a formal position on the abortion issue have generally regarded abortion as a matter for the conscience of the individual and her family.[3]

When I first read this, I could not believe that a significant number of Protestants ever believed that "life does not begin until live birth." Such a belief seems absolutely foreign to Scripture, where we read, for example, that John the Baptist, still in his mother's womb, leapt at the presence of the newly conceived Jesus. But my investigations confirmed that not long after the Protestant churches changed their minds on contraception, many of them compromised on abortion as well. Lutheran sociologist Allan Carlson describes well the great extent to which numerous Protestant bodies have abandoned the traditional Christian view of the sanctity of life. If Martin Luther, a fierce opponent of contraception and abortion, were alive today, Carlson writes, he would discover that his Protestant heirs had embraced contraception and abortion as compatible with Christian ethics by the 1960s. Protestant leaders condemned Pope Paul VI's opposition to both acts in the 1968 encyclical, *Humanae Vitae*, as an attempt to impose "Catholic views" on the world. Although mainline Protestant leaders clearly led the charge, their evangelical counterparts were not far behind. A month after the pope issued his encyclical, an evangelical symposium sponsored by *Christianity Today* and the Christian Medical Society came to the defense of contraception and, in some cases, abortion: "The Christian physician will advise induced abortion only to safeguard greater values sanctioned by Scripture. These values should include individual health, family values, and social responsibility." . . . Five years later, Southern Baptist voices even defended the 1973 *Roe v. Wade* decision that legalized abortion. W. A. Criswell, for example, claimed: "I have always felt that it was only after the child was born and had life separate from its mother that it became an individual person." . . .

In 1970, a task force encouraged what is now the Presbyterian Church (U.S.A.) to reject the old "taboos and prohibitions" and to give her blessing to "mass contraceptive techniques," homosexuality, and low-cost abortion on demand. The same year, the Lutheran Church in America fully embraced contraception and abortion as responsible choices. Finally, in 1977, the United Church of Christ . . . declared free access to contraception and abortion as matters of justice.[4]

All who fight for life should take the lessons of history to heart. As long as the contraceptive mentality prevails, abortion will follow. One of the most practical steps we can take to combat abortion is to renounce contraception in our homes.

In a culture of death, married Christians must reclaim the true meaning and beauty of sex, not only by bearing and rearing children, but by forsaking contraception and demonstrating purity, chastity, and restraint. As the Chinese philosopher Confucius said of those who desired cultural renewal in his day, "Wanting good government in their states, they first established order in their own families; wanting order in the home, they first disciplined themselves."[5]

If you can control your own body only by destroying another person's body, then control has come much too late. — WENDELL BERRY

A Bitter Pill

THERE IS ANOTHER troubling reason why abortion will not end as long as the contraceptive mentality prevails: some "contraceptives" actually cause abortions. The intrauterine device (IUD), "morning-after pills," and "emergency contraceptives" are in fact abortifacients, which work primarily after conception by preventing a fertilized egg from implanting in the uterus. There are also good reasons to believe that Norplant, Depo-Provera, and even the most popular contraceptive of all, the Pill, sometimes work as abortifacients.

During Attorney General John Ashcroft's confirmation hearings, *People* magazine ran a story on George W. Bush's controversial nominee. Feminist organizations opposed Ashcroft, the popular magazine reported, because

> As a senator Ashcroft drafted a highly restrictive Constitutional amendment that would have allowed for terminating a pregnancy only to save the life of the mother. . . . What's more, Ashcroft's amendment proposed defining life as starting at fertilization, an interpretation that abortion rights advocates argue would, in effect, outlaw birth control measures such as the pill, which can rely on blocking the development of a fertilized egg.[1]

It was only a month or two before the Ashcroft hearings that Bethany and I first discovered what abortion advocates have long known: that if you oppose abortion on the grounds that life begins at conception, you must oppose also the Pill, which can prevent the implantation of a fertilized egg — a tiny, genetically complete human being.[2]

The Pill comes in two basic types: one is a combination of the synthetic hormones estrogen and progestin, while the other, known as the "minipill," contains only progestin. One of progestin's primary effects is to thin the lining of the uterus (called the endometrium). Within the first two weeks after conception, a newly fertilized egg must implant in the endometrium in order to live — otherwise it is flushed out of the uterus and aborted. By thinning the uterine lining considerably, the Pill renders the endometrium hostile to implantation, making it difficult for a fertilized egg to survive.

Combination estrogen/progestin pills work in three ways: by suppressing ovulation, thickening cervical mucus to impede sperm travel, and thinning the uterine lining to prevent implantation. The first two mechanisms are contraceptive, while the third is abortifacient. Progestin-only pills rarely suppress ovulation, and rely more exclusively on thickening cervical mucus and thinning the uterine lining.[3] Women on both types of pill can still ovulate (more frequently with the progestin-only pill), and sperm can still reach the egg, despite the thickened mucus; when conception occurs, the fertilized egg will face a hostile endometrium, much like a seed falling on rocky, nutrient-depleted soil.[4] Walter Larimore and Randy Alcorn document:

> Magnetic Resonance Imaging (MRI) reveals that the endometrial lining of Pill users is constantly thinner than that of nonusers — up to 58 percent thinner. Recent and fairly sophisticated ultrasound studies have all concluded that endometrial thickness is related to the "functional receptivity" of the endometrium in women. . . . Other studies have shown that when the lining of the uterus becomes too thin, implantation of the pre-born child (called the blastocyst or pre-embryo at this stage) does not occur. The loss of a pre-born child is obviously abortifacient.

The minimal endometrial thickness required to maintain a pregnancy ranges from 5 to 13 mm, whereas the average endometrial thickness in women on the Pill is only 1.1 mm.[5]

How many babies are denied implantation because of the Pill? We can't know for sure, but even one would be too many.

The medical literature describing how the Pill and other hormonal contraceptives can cause abortions is widely available. Even so, many pro-life Christians still use the Pill, and many pro-life pastors still recommend it to young couples. Why is this?

First, some Christians believe that life begins at implantation, not conception, and that drugs and devices that prevent implantation are thus morally acceptable.[6] This position seems problematic for several reasons. Scientifically, to say that life begins at implantation, or any other point after conception, is to draw an arbitrary line. A fertilized egg undergoes no substantial change upon implantation, just as a fetus undergoes no substantial change upon birth. After conception, the progression from embryo to fetus to child to adult is continuous, and all the genetic information necessary for development is contained in the fertilized egg. Moreover, there is no biblical evidence to support the notion that God breathes the soul into the body at some point in between conception and birth. A newly fertilized egg is a human body, however small, and wherever there is a living human body there must be a soul. As the Epistle of St. James states, "the body without the spirit is dead" (2:26). To assert otherwise is to slip into dualism, reducing the body to a mere envelope for the soul. In the Scriptures, body and soul are separated only by death, which is what makes death so horrible.

Second, many pro-life Christians, while believing that life begins at conception, have been misled by confusing terminology used in the scientific literature on contraceptives. In 1976, the American College of Obstetricians and Gynecologists redefined pregnancy as beginning at the successful implantation of a fertilized egg.[7] Under this definition, abortifacient drugs that prevent implantation are labeled as contraceptives. The *Chicago Tribune* recently ran an article on "emergency contraception." According to the *Tribune*, emergency contraception is "basically a double dose of regular birth control pills within 72 hours of [intercourse], followed by another double dose 12 hours later. That regimen can significantly reduce the risk of pregnancy by . . . keeping a fertilized egg from implanting in the womb."[8] If life begins at conception, however, this is not the prevention of pregnancy but the termination of pregnancy. (It's also important to note how the *Tribune* story validates the thesis that the Pill can cause abortions; a mere double-dose of regular birth control pills can thin the uterine lining almost instantly, rendering it unable to support life.)

Third, some Protestant leaders, despite having heard the evidence, choose to believe that the Pill does not prevent implantation. James Dobson, founder of Focus on the Family, affirms that life begins at conception but finds the evidence that the Pill causes abortions unconvincing. To be fair to this view, and out of respect for their good work in many other areas, I will quote the core of Focus on the Family's official position statement on the Pill and other hormonal contraceptives.

> The most commonly prescribed birth control pills, called "combined" oral contraceptives, contain both estrogen and progesterone. These medications, as well as Depo-Provera injections, seem to work primarily through suppression of ovulation. They also cause the mucus at the opening of the uterus to be thickened and, therefore, less likely to be penetrated by sperm. If combined oral contraceptives and Depo-Provera work only through these mechanisms, they are functioning as true contraceptives because they prevent the sperm and egg from uniting. However, there is controversy as to whether they also bring about changes (primar-ily within the uterus) that could increase the likelihood of losing a fertilized egg if ovulation and conception should occur.
>
> Pro-life physicians who have carefully and conscientiously

studied this issue have come to different conclusions regarding the interpretation and implications of the relevant scientific data. After two years of extended deliberation and prayer, the PRC [Focus on the Family's Physicians Research Council] has not been able to reach a consensus as to the likelihood, or even the possibility, that these medications might contribute to the loss of human life after fertilization. The majority of the experts to which Dr. Dobson has spoken feel that the pill does not have an abortifacient effect. A minority of the experts feel that when conception occurs on the pill, there is enough of a possibility for an abortifacient effect, however remote, to warrant informing women about it.[9]

Given Focus on the Family's longstanding commitment to the unborn, it seems odd that they will not heed the minority report and warn couples even of the *possibility* that the Pill causes abortions. The language of their statement expresses uncertainty: "may be evidence," "problematic," "seem to work," "there is controversy as to whether," "a majority of experts feel." Given such uncertainty, wouldn't it be better to err on the side of life?

But are things really so uncertain? Is there really a great "controversy" as to whether hormonal contraceptives thin the endometrium, making it hostile to implantation? Outside of Christian circles, I haven't found any. Bethany and I searched the Internet and scoured the shelves of the local Barnes & Noble, reading everything we could find on the Pill, checking the authoritative pharmaceutical guides (including the *Physicians Desk Reference*), peer-reviewed medical journals, and consumer health organizations. Everywhere we looked, we found the same conclusion: all forms of the Pill thin the uterine lining to prevent implantation.

We must be sensitive on this point because many Christian women use the Pill, and many Christian doctors prescribe it. I am not calling their character into question. But when pre-born children are at stake, how can we ignore the overwhelming consensus in the pharmaceutical literature about how the Pill works? In order to claim that the Pill never acts as an abortifacient, one has to discredit all of the sources that doctors and patients normally rely on for their pharmaceutical information. One must believe that these authorities actually want us to think abortions are taking place when they aren't, something they have no vested interest in doing because most don't believe a fertilized egg is a person. Faced with this evidence, why take the risk?

PART THREE

Bethany

The home is the schoolhouse for affection wherein a mother completes the work that was begun when the child was born.

— FULTON J. SHEEN

How can it be a large career to tell other people's children about the Rule of Three, and a small career to tell one's own children about the Universe? How can it be broad to be the same thing to everyone, and narrow to be everything to someone? No; a woman's function is laborious, because it is gigantic, not because it is minute.

— G. K. CHESTERTON

Just a Mom

"HOW MANY OF YOU want to be at-home moms?" The question, from my tenth-grade English teacher, was directed at the females in the room. We made up over half of the class of twenty-five sophomores. I proudly raised my hand, then waited for at least a few others to join me. The room was completely still. Everyone stared at me.

By the time I went to college, not much had changed. Marriage was closer than ever for my peers, yet only a few of the young women I knew admitted they would postpone a career for children. Those who did confided in me only after I told them of my own feelings. They seemed relieved to find a contemporary who didn't mock their desire.

When I finally got the nerve up to tell my college advisor that what I really wanted to do with my life was to get married and be a mom, I watched his expression go from surprise to dismay to disapproval. "I wouldn't have expected you to be that type," he said, shaking his head and looking at me with great disappointment. "You just seem so . . . involved."

He paused, then asked in a hushed, sad voice, "Is it pressure from your boyfriend?" A laugh escaped me before I could stop it — his tone was the same as if he had asked me if my boyfriend was abusive.

"No," I informed him. At the time — a year before I met my husband — I didn't have a boyfriend. Despite my desire to get married, I was not at college to hunt down a husband.

Many of my teachers and classmates wondered why I was in college if I "just" wanted to be a wife and mom. That question always irked me. I love to learn and want to have a wealth of knowledge to impart to my children. Why shouldn't a housewife be educated? I want to equip myself and hone my skills to the point of craft.

My mother earned her degree in elementary education twenty years ago and promptly became a housemom after graduating. Since then my brother, sisters, and I have been her highest priority, but during the tight times she helped out by substitute teaching. Though we didn't like having her gone, she was able to alleviate some of the burden my father carried. I will be glad to do this for my own husband if the need ever arises.

If God gives you children, be a mother with your whole mind, soul, and strength. If he has given you the talents to be an engineer, the same thing applies. But I am dubious that he would ever ask us to be fully both at one time. Women my age seem to think that we will have enough time and energy to do and be everything — be full-time wife, mother, and career woman all rolled into one.

I agree that God wants us to use and enjoy the talents he's given us, but he never promised us inexhaustible resources. He created us with limitations and placed only twenty-four hours in a day. We cannot expect to juggle all the hats and be the best we can be at all of them. The reality is that if I choose to have a full-time career, my husband and kids will have me only part-time.

Danielle Crittenden makes an excellent observation in *What Our Mothers Didn't Tell Us:* that quality time with kids can't be scheduled into a day.[1] Children want a mother's presence, the knowledge that she will be there when they have a question or a story to tell — but quite often they simply want her to do her own work while they color and play with pals.

And those memorable times — their first steps and words, their profound utterances of child wisdom, the moments of belly laughing together — happen at the most unexpected times during day-in, day-out living. The chances are much higher that a mother will miss out on them if she is flying to California on a business trip — or even if she is five miles away in a classroom teaching everyone else's children.

I can guess what most people think when they find out about my lack of career aspirations. They picture me in ten years:

dressed in sweats doing laundry for my four kids; my degree collecting dust somewhere on a bookshelf; living in a one-income-sized home; driving a used minivan.

They imagine my peers, by contrast, employing their education to the fullest. Unfettered by familial life, thanks to day care, public schools, and extracurricular activities, they will naturally be rewarded with financial and material gain — but at what cost to their husbands and children?

Having a parent at home is crucial for a young child's well-being. If at all possible, the ideal is to have both parents home most of the time; in our modern society, however, this goal is difficult to attain. Usually, the husband works outside of the home, because a mother is biologically designed to be the primary caregiver during a child's early years — she's the one who carries him inside her and nurses him after he's born. Consequently, a mother will have a greater inbuilt desire to be close to her baby, and a baby will benefit more from her immediate presence than from a father's — most obviously, because men cannot breastfeed. (In the *Journal of the American*

Medical Association, a doctor who studied the health benefits of breastfeeding recently lamented that many women stop breastfeeding too soon because they return to the workforce.[2]) Still, a father should strive to be home for as many hours a day as possible. Motherhood is a large task, and stay-at-home moms can easily be overwhelmed. It's important to have your husband, friends, and relatives all helping out. Once the children are about school-age, some fathers might choose to stay at home while the mother works.

The Christian life is about sacrifices, giving up certain things for the sake of greater long-term benefits. I'm bringing up the subject of full-time, at-home mothering in a book about contraception because they are closely related. Careerism — centering life around work, not home — is one of the main reasons men and women view pregnancy as a threat and rely on contraception to prevent it. Christians should have an entirely different view of life's purpose than the surrounding culture. Ours is a life of sacrifice, to be molded after Christ's. Both husbands and wives are called to sacrifice their immediate sexual desires for the good of their union; to sacrifice financial success for the sake of welcoming new life; to sacrifice their vocational and personal priorities for the sake of being excellent parents. Our lives are to be poured out for others in love.

Sacrifices don't usually come easily. There may be times of financial strain in our marriage. I might encounter tension with my married female peers because I choose to stay at home. Sam and I will both have to give up a lot of personal time; there will be nights we're itching to read a big fat novel in one sitting instead of reciting *Hop on Pop* for the fiftieth time to the kids.

It is only by sacrifice that we understand what true love, commitment, and maturity really mean. Being a husband and father, or wife and mother, forces you to look outside yourself to the needs of others. I'm not saying that I relish changing diapers and cleaning up burpy blankets, but there is a certain amount of joy involved that transcends the self — an awareness that makes the smells and uncleanliness bearable. That joy is akin to the pleasure shared between two lovers, when you cannot determine where your own happiness ends and the other's begins.

You are making this little person you love more comfortable, contented, and clean.

I want my children to know that they are more important to me than a career. Because of the choices my mom made when she was little older than I, my younger siblings are reaping the benefits of having a full-time mom, one who is available for conversation, hugs, and laughs (and a healthy number of arguments about chores) any time of day.

I am attempting to give that gift to our own children. If it means I drive a beat-up car and shop at thrift stores for the rest of my life, so be it. Little kids don't know the difference between Goodwill and GAP. I certainly didn't.

We will raise both our sons and our daughters with the knowledge that they have full abilities to be and do all that God wants, in their wholeness in Christ, in their education — and in the delightful duties that may come with being a woman, wife, and mother, or being a man, husband, and father.

A friend of mine once said his greatest desire is to create

something beautiful and lasting. That stuck with me. I'm working to create a beautiful and lasting marriage with Sam, and with him I want to continue to bear and rear children, which are the most exquisite and eternal creations we humans can take part in fashioning. The Bible is clear that sons and daughters are among the greatest blessings we will ever receive. Architects design buildings that will someday fall down, programmers construct computer software that will eventually be obsolete — but fathers and mothers create and cultivate souls that will never die. How wonderful to experience just an inkling of what God feels as our Father.

When I am old and I look at my wrinkled hands, I want to know that the creases came from — among many things — years of playing music, reading books, drawing pictures, and writing stories. But my greatest hope is that those lines will remind me most of hours spent washing my babies' and grandbabies' tummies, tucking them into bed, and teaching them what I have learned.

At the dawn of salvation, it is the birth of a child which is proclaimed as joyful news. . . . The source of this "great joy" is the birth of the Savior, but Christmas also reveals the full meaning of every human birth, and the joy which accompanies the birth of the Messiah is thus seen to be the foundation and fulfillment of joy at every child born into the world.

— POPE JOHN PAUL II

All love tends to an incarnation, even God's.

— FULTON J. SHEEN

Be Not Afraid

A FEW DAYS before Christmas Eve, I was curled up next to
Sam in a barn, bundled thoroughly to keep out the chill
of December. My gangly younger brother, who has sprouted to
my height, came and sprawled across my lap with his arms around
my neck to keep us both warm.

The people of the Christian community I grew up with were
all around us. We were observing an annual tradition — sacri-
ficing our body temperature for a short half-hour in order to
remember the birth of Christ, in as authentic a setting as you
can get in Wisconsin.

My mother stood front and center, with a lone cow and a few chickens and ducks in the pen behind her. Six little girls, ages six to eight, perched on a row of hay bales in front of us. With haphazard cardboard wings duct-taped to their bulky coats and circlets of tinsel on their bare heads, they waited shyly in the limelight for their big moment.

My mother read of Gabriel's announcement. "And coming in, he said to her, 'Hail, favored one! The Lord is with you.' But she was greatly troubled at this statement, and kept pondering what kind of salutation this might be. And the angel said to her, 'Be not afraid.'"

"Be not afraid!" Nettie said in a strong voice. "Be not afraid!" Rosie echoed. "Be not afraid!" continued Ellie, their adopted sister. "Be not afraid," quietly, from my cousin Callie. "Be not afraid," coyly, from my cousin Amy. "Be not afraid," in a carefully pronounced whisper from my little friend Edona, a Kosovar refugee.

My mother continued with Joseph's dilemma, as, unbeknownst

to her, Lucia the Brown Swiss cow nibbled on her scarf. "An angel of the Lord appeared to him in a dream, saying, 'Joseph, son of David, *be not afraid* to take Mary as your wife.'"

The echo of small voices chorused once again down the line. "Be not afraid." Their performance was endearing, but the full magnitude of their simple phrase hadn't yet registered with me.

It was Christmas Eve when my first solid assurance of the miracle came. I was curled up on my parents' bed talking to my mother about menopause. Hot flashes came up — she said they were typical at two times in life: when you're pregnant, and when you're starting menopause.

"What does a hot flash feel like?" I asked, trying to be subtle, but probably failing thoroughly.

"Like a wave of fever that comes and goes," she said. "You wake up in the middle of the night and suddenly the covers are cloistering."

I swallowed, left the room, and went to find Sam. He was seated at the computer doing research for an article. "You know how when you hug me sometimes you say I feel really hot?" He looked at me over his shoulder. "That must be when I'm having a hot flash — and my mom said that only happens when you're pregnant." He turned with a look on his face as if the Christmas tree lights had just been plugged in. I don't see my calm, steady mate wearing that sort of expression very often.

Sam was happy. I was scared. Not because I didn't want the baby — I had wanted this child since I was old enough to carry a baby doll. Not because I was young — I was nineteen, but the wait had already felt too long. Not because it was too soon — Sam and I both knew it was the best thing that could happen to our marriage, a crowning blessing we were not worthy to receive. Not because my family would disapprove — my brother already asked me hopefully every time he talked to me on the phone, "Are you pregnant yet?" (and we had been married only three weeks).

I was scared of so many things that are hard to verbalize. Perhaps it was just the initiation into womanhood, with all the self-giving that life entails. I was opening myself up to inevitable hurt — whether it came at the death of this child in a week's time or whether it was stretched out into sixty years of having pieces of my soul pulling at me from the separate beings of my children.

I was restless that night. I felt bad that I wasn't excited enough, worried about telling people I had gotten pregnant on my honeymoon, and so on — even as I rationally fought the emotions. When I awoke the next morning, the fear crept back, alongside the memory of my almost-certain pregnancy.

Sam put his hand over my tummy and prayed a blessing on the baby. He knew what I was feeling; I had kept him up late the night before, spilling it all.

"Still scared?" he asked.

I nodded, and he put his hand on my cheek. "Remember? *Be not afraid.* The Lord is with you."

The memory of the girls' voices came back. *Be not afraid. Be not afraid. Be not afraid.* It echoed over and over inside me. Funny how that whole story had never been alive to me before. Now, I involuntarily savored a tinge of Mary's feelings. I was participating in the act that had linked women to God since our creation.

I had (and have) no guarantees that there aren't reasons to fear. Mary was instructed to "be not afraid" despite the fact that she was ultimately to watch her son tortured to death. The fear I felt that Christmas still comes and goes, as I'm sure it will for the rest of my life. To be a mother is a constant battle to trust God. A hard thing to do, when I'm fully aware that God never promises lack of pain. I don't trust him to prevent my children from dying during my lifetime. All I can do is vaguely trust him to somehow carry me through whatever is ahead — and I can bless his name for giving me children at all. None of this is my right, not even the breath I take from his air. I am to humbly accept the joys of life, wait patiently through the sorrows, and ultimately use the short time I have here in preparation for an eternity without tears.

To be with child is to be blessed among women. "The mother

is both the physical preserver of life and the moral provider of truth; she is nature's constant challenge to death, the bearer of cosmic plenitude, the herald of eternal realities, God's greatest cooperator."[1]

To all married couples, I echo: *Be not afraid.* The Lord is with you.

Our natural reason looks at marriage and turns up its nose and says, "Alas! Must I rock the baby? wash its diapers? make its bed? smell its stench? stay up nights with it? take care of it when it cries? heal its rashes and sores? and on top of that care for my spouse, provide labor at my trade, take care of this and take care of that? . . .

What then does the Christian faith say to this? It opens its eyes, looks upon all these insignificant, distasteful, and despised duties in the spirit, and is aware that they are all adorned with divine approval as with the costliest gold and jewels. It says, "O God, I confess I am not worthy to rock that little babe or wash its diapers, or to be entrusted with the care of a child and its mother. How is it that I without any merit have come to this distinction of being certain that I am serving thy creature and thy most precious will? Oh, how gladly I will do so."

—— MARTIN LUTHER

Having Babies, Not Regrets

A YOUNG MOTHER sent me this note in reponse to an article I wrote about motherhood: "Having children is one thing I never tell any married couple to wait for. The Bible says 'children are an heritage of the Lord; blessed is the man whose quiver is full of them.' Are we going to believe God's word or not?"

It's all too easy to see this wondrous gift as an everyday commonality, to lose the reverence for the mystery of conception. Young couples figure they have the rest of their lives to raise kids, and they should spend their youth and strength on pursuing education, money, and careers. In actuality, they may be wasting the prime years for starting a family — God designed our bodies to be the most healthy and strong for bearing and raising children from around ages eighteen to twenty-seven.

I've had married people tell me that they prayed about using contraception and God gave them the go-ahead. I'm skeptical of such statements because I know, from my own experience, that we often hear "God's voice" as filtered through our own cultural conditioning.

God does have a different plan for every person. Some marry young, some marry older, and some never marry at all. (Both Jesus and the apostle Paul tell us that singleness for the sake of the kingdom of heaven is a high calling, worthy of our greatest respect.[1]) But whether single or married, barren or fertile, God wants us to spend our lives loving others. These include babies, children, friends, strangers, the sick, the elderly, family, and foreigners. If you are single or barren, you have an opportunity to channel your love into lonely people (both children and adults) that others are too busy to care for.

Barren couples will tell you just how miraculous children are. It's easy for those of us who are fertile to lose sight of the truth that each child is a miracle. Too often, we treat them as casual commodities to be obtained "in a few years." We act as though we have complete control over our bodies, and we think fertility can be turned on and off like a light switch. When we're finally "ready" to have kids, we feel that we have a *right* to them. If God doesn't give them to us, we try to manufacture them, discarding any "extra" or "unfit" embryos along the way.

I know our elders are well-meaning when they advise us to use contraception and put off having kids, but I don't think they realize the fruit of their attitudes. In their view, children are often reduced to mere consumers that we must be financially prepared to supply, or romance-robbing scamps that wreak havoc on marital intimacy.

Sam and I want our children to know we desired them to the extent that we sacrificed our "getting to know each other" years in order to meet them. We are trying to lay the groundwork now to secure in their hearts that they are, and always will be, our top priority. There may be times ahead in our marriage when another pregnancy feels more like a punishment than a blessing. It's easy to get bogged down in life and lose an eternal perspective.

But I have never heard a Christian parent say, "You know, I really regret having that fifth child," or, "I wish I hadn't had any children at all." I have heard regrets from those who chose not to have more children when they were able to, and sorrow from those who have always been barren. I have read many stories of Christian couples who gave up contraception — none regret it. To welcome a child, after all, is to welcome Christ.

"And [Jesus] called a child to Himself and set him before them, and said, 'Truly I say to you, . . . whoever receives one such child in My name receives Me'" (Matthew 18:2-5).

RESOURCES

OUR MAIN PURPOSE in writing this book is to encourage readers to examine for themselves the facts about contraception and Natural Family Planning. Though we've tried to explain the philosophy behind NFP, we haven't provided any practical instruction in NFP methods.

To learn more about NFP, a great place to start is the Couple to Couple League. Visit their Web site (www.ccli.org), call (513) 471-2000, or write to the Couple to Couple League International, P.O. Box 111184, Cincinnati, OH 45211-1184. The League offers many services for its members, including NFP instruction by certified "teaching couples" across the country; a home study course; fertility counseling and evaluation of charts; a bi-monthly newsletter; and more.

Two further organizations for NFP instruction are WOOMB International (www.woomb.org) and Family of the Americas Foundation (www.familyplanning.net), both of which teach the Billings Ovulation Method of NFP, developed by doctors John and Evelyn Billings of Australia. This method differs from the "sympto-thermal" method taught by the Couple to Couple League in that only the primary sign of fertility, the presence of cervical fluid, is tracked. The manual published by the Family of the Americas Foundation, Mercedes Arzú Wilson's *Love & Fertility*, is the simplest presentation of NFP we've seen — it's written on a level that a high school student could easily grasp. If you are interested in taking an NFP course, find out which organizations offer classes in your area and sift through their materials to see which looks best for you.

Many women use the Pill not to prevent pregnancy but to

regulate their cycle. In most cases, however, proper nutrition and vitamin supplements will provide the needed balance naturally, with no harmful side effects. To learn more about how nutrition affects menstrual cycles and fertility, we highly recommend Marilyn M. Shannon's *Fertility, Cycles and Nutrition*, available in its third edition from the Couple to Couple League.

For an in-depth look at the theology of the human person, marriage, and NFP, please see Mary Shivanandan's *Crossing the Threshold of Love: A New Vision of Marriage* (The Catholic University of America Press, 1999). We read this while we were engaged, and we cannot imagine a better book for premarital counseling. An excellent Bible study based on Shivanandan's book is available from Women Affirming Life (www.affirmlife.com).

Shivanandan's book focuses on the thought and writings of Karol Wojtyla, the man who became Pope John Paul II. The Pope's writings on marriage, family, and the sanctity of life are of vital importance for all Christians. To pick just one of his books, we'd recommend *Love & Responsibility* (Ignatius Press,

1993). Those who believe the Pope is somehow "anti-pleasure" or "anti-women" would do well to read this extraordinary book, which was originally published in Poland in 1960.

Regarding the Pill and how it works, a comprehensive and objective study is Randy Alcorn's *Does the Birth Control Pill Cause Abortions?* (Eternal Perspective Ministries, 2000). Alcorn's book is available on-line at www.epm.org/bcp.html.

Finally, two valuable Web sites: The American Life League (www.all.org) posts well-reasoned articles on many life-related topics, from contraception to euthanasia. More great essays are available at Life Issues (www.lifeissues.net), which is particularly strong on bioethical issues such as embryonic stem cell research and human cloning.

NOTES

FOREWORD

1. Unless otherwise noted, all scriptural quotations in the foreword are taken from the New International Version of the Bible and those in the rest of the book from the New American Standard Bible.

2. G. K. Chesterton, *What's Wrong With the World* (San Francisco: Ignatius Press, 1994), p. 143.

PRECONCEIVED NOTIONS

1. See Allan Carlson, "The Peril of Statistics: Pregnant Teenagers and the Retreat from Marriage," *The Family in America*, Volume 13, Number 7 (July 1999), pp. 3–4, where Carlson writes,

The real news in the [1997 National Center for Health Statistics] report was the decline in the overall U.S. fertility rate to 14.5 per 1000 population, the lowest figure ever recorded in our nation's history. And *all* of this decrease comes among married women. While the number of out-of-wedlock births remains at historic highs . . . the number of births to married women has fallen by 13 percent since 1990.

See also Carlson's, "An Elegy for the Free Sexual World," *The Family in America*, Volume 13, Number 7 (July 1999), pp. 1–3. Carlson writes,

Fertile young adults rely on mechanical devices and chemical agents to thwart the designs of nature. In places as culturally different as Spain, Italy, Denmark, and Germany, the sexual experimentation starts early, but hardly anyone brings forth a child. Total fertility rates (TFR) in these lands (which must reach an average of 2.1 children per woman if they are just to replace the current generation) hover near 1.2. Projected forward two generations, nearly 60 percent of these nations' children will be without siblings, cousins, uncles, or aunts.

IMAGO DEI

1. Quoted in Vladimir Lossky, *The Mystical Theology of the Eastern Church* (Crestwood, New York: St. Vladimir's Seminary Press, 1976), p. 116.
2. "Letter of His Holiness Pope John Paul II to Artists" (4 April 1999). Available on-line at: www.vatican.va/holy_father/john_paul_ii/letters.

3. Kallistos Ware, *The Orthodox Way* (Crestwood, New York: St. Vladimir's Seminary Press, 1995), p. 120.

ONE FLESH

1. Alexander Schmemann, *For the Life of the World* (New York: National Student Christian Federation, 1963), p. 64.

2. Mary Shivanandan, *Crossing the Threshold of Love: A New Vision of Marriage* (Washington, D.C.: The Catholic University of America Press, 1999), p. 274.

3. Doris Betts, *Souls Raised from the Dead* (New York: Scribner Paperback Fiction, 1995), p. 53.

BODY LANGUAGE

1. Sarah E. Hinlicky, "Contraception: A Symposium," *First Things* 88 (December 1998), p. 22.

2. See, for example, Gilbert Meilaender and Phillip Turner, "Contraception: A Symposium," *First Things* 88 (December 1998), pp. 22-24.

INTENDED FOR PLEASURE?

1. Tim and Beverly LaHaye, *The Act of Marriage: The Beauty of Sexual Love* (Grand Rapids: Zondervan, 1998), p. 265.

2. Tony Campolo, *Following Jesus Without Embarrassing God* (Dallas: Word, 1997), pp. 232–33.

3. Bob and Gerri Laird, "Birth Control: It Almost Cost Us Our Marriage," available on-line at www.ccli.org/articles/bcmar.shtml.

4. Wendell Berry, *The Unsettling of America: Culture & Agriculture*, third edition (San Francisco: Sierra Club Books, 1996), p. 132.

IN THE FAMILY WAY

1. See Sheila Matgen Kippley, *Breastfeeding and Natural Child Spacing: How Ecological Breastfeeding Spaces Babies* (Cincinnati: The Couple to Couple League International, 1999).

2. Tim and Beverly LaHaye, *The Act of Marriage: The Beauty of Sexual Love* (Grand Rapids: Zondervan, 1998), p. 269.

3. Elisabeth Elliot, "Christian Stewardship and Natural Family Planning," unpublished lecture delivered at the International *Humanae Vitae* Conference, 1993.

4. www.plannedparenthood.org/bc/WaysToChart.HTM.

5. Toni Weschler, *Taking Charge of Your Fertility: The Definitive Guide to Natural Birth Control and Pregnancy Achievement* (New York: Harper Perennial Library, 1995), pp. 33–34.

6. Weschler, *Taking Charge of Your Fertility*, p. 217.

7. Gregory Popcak, "Does Using NFP Guarantee the Success of a Marriage?" *CCL Family Foundations*, Volume XXVII, Number 4 (January/February 2001), pp. 28–29.

8. R. F. (anonymous), "Protestant Couple Eager to Learn a Better Way," *CCL Family Foundations*, Volume XXVII, Number 3 (November/December 2000), p. 7.

9. Elliot, "Christian Stewardship and Natural Family Planning."

OF TRAINS & TRADITION

1. Quoted in Celeste McGovern, "Brave New World" column, *Alberta Report*, 20 November 2000.

2. Andrea Tone, *Devices and Desires: A history of Contraceptives in America* (New York: Hill and Wang, 2001), p. 13.

3. John A. Hardon, *The Catholic Catechism: A Contemporary Catechism of the Teachings of the Catholic Church* (New York: Doubleday & Company, 1975), p. 367.

4. Hippolytus, *Refutation of All Heresies* 9:12 (A.D. 225).

5. Epiphanius of Salamis, *Medicine Chest Against Heresies* 26:5:2 (A.D. 375).

6. John Chrysostom, *Homilies on Matthew* 28:5 (A.D. 391).

7. John Chrysostom, *Homilies on Romans* 24 (A.D. 391).

8. Quoted in Allan Carlson, "The Ironic Protestant Reversal: How the Original Family Movement Swallowed the Pill," *Family Policy*, Volume 12, Number 5 (September/October 1999), pp. 16–21.

FROM CONTRACEPTION TO ABORTION

1. *Roe v. Wade*, 410 US 113 (1973), Opinion of the Court, section VII. The complete texts of all Supreme Court cases cited in this chapter are available

on-line at the Constitutional Law and Abortion Web site (http://members. aol.com/abtrbng/conlaw.htm).

2. *Planned Parenthood v. Casey*, 505 US 833 (1992), Opinion of the Court, section II.

3. *Roe v. Wade*, Opinion of the Court, section IX.

4. Allan Carlson, "The Ironic Protestant Reversal: How the Original Family Movement Swallowed the Pill," *Family Policy*, Volume 12, Number 5 (September/October 1999), pp. 16–21.

5. Quoted in Wendell Berry, *The Unsettling of America: Culture & Agriculture*, third edition (San Francisco: Sierra Club Books, 1996), p. 16.

A BITTER PILL

1. Bill Hewitt and Rose Ellen O'Connor, "Playing for Keeps," *People Weekly*, Volume 55, Number 3 (22 January 2001), pp. 56–61.

2. William L. Saunders, "Disposable Human Beings?" *Family Policy*, Volume 13, Number 6 (November/December 2000), pp. 1–6, 16–18. Saunders writes:

> . : . [L]ife begins upon the fertilization of an oocyte or "egg" by a single sperm cell. Before the point of fertilization, neither the sperm nor the oocyte . . . is a human being. Left alone, without union with the other, neither sperm nor oocyte could develop into a human being; each would simply die. However, once they are fused together, the "fertilized egg" will develop continuously until it becomes a fully-grown human being. . . .

> With forty-six chromosomes, the "fertilized egg" is more than a simple cell like the sperm or the oocyte — it is a living human being. If given nutrition and a hospitable environment, the fertilized egg will live and develop. . . . Equipped with forty-six chromosomes, it *genetically* directs its own development. That growth is continuous, and, though it is significant change, it is not what philosophers call *substantial* change - — no change of *nature* from one kind of being into another.

3. According to the U.S. Food and Drug Administration's Web site, "Mini-pills [progestin-only Pills] . . . work by reducing and thickening cervical mucus to prevent sperm from reaching the egg. They also keep the uterine lining from thickening, which prevents a fertilized egg from implanting in the uterus" (www.fda.gov/fdac/features/1997/397_baby.html).

4. Planned Parenthood's Web site states: "Both types of pill [combination and progestin-only] can . . . prevent fertilized eggs from implanting in the uterus" (www.plannedparenthood.org/bc/YOU_AND_PILL.HTM). According to the *American Medical Association Encyclopedia of Medicine* (New York: Random House, 1989), p. 305, "All hormone contraceptives . . . cause thinning of the endometrium (lining of the uterus)." And the *Physician's Desk Reference Family Guide to Women's Health* gives this summary:

> Suppression of ovulation is the main mode by which OCs [oral contraceptives, i.e. the Pill] and Depo-Provera prevent pregnancy . . . . Even if ovulation and fertilization do take place, hormonal methods provide another measure of protection: changes to the uterine lining. Normally, estrogen initiates the thickening of the lining of the uterus in the first

part of the cycle, while progesterone kicks in later to help the lining mature. Since both hormones are present throughout the pill cycle, and progestin is supplied continuously by implants and the shot, the usual hormonal variations are masked and the lining rarely has a chance to develop enough to nurture a fertilized egg." (quoted on HealthSquare.com, www.healthsqr.com/fgwh/which21.htm)

5. Walter L. Larimore and Randy Alcorn, "Using the Birth Control Pill Is Ethically Unacceptable," in John F. Kilner, Paige C. Cunningham, and W. David Hager, editors, *The Reproduction Revolution: A Christian Appraisal of Sexuality, Reproductive Technologies, and the Family* (Grand Rapids: Eerdmans, 2000), pp. 179–91.

6. This position is cautiously advocated by Gilbert Meilaender, a leading Protestant bioethicist, in *Bioethics: A Primer for Christians* (Grand Rapids/ Cambridge, U.K.: Wm. B. Eerdmans Publishing Co., 1996). In his chapter on abortion, Meilaender writes, ". . . there are some good reasons . . . why we might fix the beginning of human life slightly later than conception."
  These reasons are twofold. First,

   the fertilized ovum must successfully implant in the uterus before pregnancy is established, and research seems to indicate that as many as half of fertilized ova may fail to successfully implant. If any figure even approaching that is accurate, and if an individual life begins at fertilization, we would be forced to conclude that half of the human race dies after a life of four to five days. Although that is logically possible, it is also rather counterintuitive.

But does the duration of a person's time on earth determine whether he was ever really human? From a human perspective, it may seem "counterintuitive" to speak of a person who lived only four days. But in the eyes of God, what is the difference between four days and four-thousand? The fact that many fertilized eggs die before implantation does not mean that they are not living human beings; nor does this mean that it is moral to deliberately prevent a fertilized egg from implanting.

Meilaender's second reason for suggesting that life does not begin at conception is that, in some instances, a fertilized egg will segment, result-ing in twins (or triplets, quadruplets, etc.). "For the first fourteen days after fertilization," he writes,

> the individuality of the developing entity is not firmly established. Up to that point, the developing blastocyst [a fertilized egg at five to seven days along] can "segment"—that is, "twinning" can occur if the one blastocyst divides into two (or more) of the same genotype. Therefore, it is difficult to argue that an individual human being exists prior to that point. If we claim that there must be at least one individual, though there may be more than one, we have difficulty explaining what has happened to that one individual if twinning occurs.

Does the possibility of a fertilized egg producing twins really mean that the fertilized egg is not human? John Finnis, professor of Law and Philosophy at Oxford University, disagrees. "Modern techniques of cloning," Finnis writes, show up the hollowness of a line of argument which has often been exploited by theologians and others wanting to justify their claim that the embryo is not a human being, or human individual, until after the time when the cells which make up the embryo have ceased to be totipotent [capable of producing twins] and have become specialized. These lines of argument are unsound for many reasons; fundamentally, the embryo, even the one or two-cell or four-cell embryo, is fully individual, with unity, identity and wholeness quite indistinguishable from its parts, even when those parts are cells which happen each to be more or less totipotent. And this is just made obvious by the fact that, as the experiments that produced Dolly the sheep established, the cell of an adult can be taken and made totipotent, so that that adult is twinned, without at all losing the individuality which in truth he or she has had from conception. (John Finnis, "Abortion and Cloning: Some New Evasions," available on-line at www.lifeissues.net/bioethics/ fin_01aborcloneevasions.html)

7. See Randy Alcorn, *Does the Birth Control Pill Cause Abortions?* (Gresham, Ore.: Eternal Perspective Ministries, 2000), p. 12.
8. Ray Long and Rick Pearson, "Lawmakers OK Plan for Rape Victims," *The Chicago Tribune*, 4 May 2001.
9. Focus on the Family, "Position Statement on Birth Control Pills and Other Hormonal Contraceptives," received via e-mail from Focus on the Family in December 2000.

JUST A MOM

1. Danielle Crittenden, *What Our Mothers Didn't Tell Us: Why Happiness Eludes the Modern Woman* (New York: Simon & Schuster, 1999).

2. Marc Kaufman, "Breast-Feeding May Cut Obesity In Childhood," *The Washington Post*, 16 May 2001, p. A01.

BE NOT AFRAID

1. Fulton J. Sheen, *Life Is Worth Living* (San Francisco: Ignatius Press, 1999), p. 51.

HAVING BABIES, NOT REGRETS

1. See Matthew 19:12 and 1 Corinthians 7:7–8, 25–34.

ACKNOWLEDGMENTS

We wish to thank Jon Pott, Hannah Timmermans, Clare Cook, J. Budziszewski, John Wilson, Candice Watters, Ken Tanner, the Baw Beesians, and everyone at *Touchstone* for their assistance and encouragement.

OPEN EMBRACE

was designed and set into type by Sam & Bethany Torode.
The text face is Centaur, designed by Bruce Rogers in 1914
and modeled on letters cut by the fifteenth-century printer
Nicolas Jenson. The italic type, originally named Arrighi,
was designed by Frederic Warde in 1925, with letters modeled
on those of the Renaissance scribe Ludovico degli Arrighi.

The cover artwork is Lovers II *by George Tooker.*